Calling All Explorers!

50 Interesting Facts about U.S. National Parks

Jasmine Stover

D1738631

Calling All Explorers!

50 Interesting Facts about U.S. National Parks

Hey there, explorer! Are you ready to embark on an exciting journey through some of the most breathtaking and wild places in America? If you've ever wondered about the mysteries of nature, the power of waterfalls, or the secrets hidden beneath the Earth's surface, get ready to be blown away!

This book is your very own treasure map of the United States National Parks. It will guide you through a world of wonder just waiting to be explored by you! So put on your adventure hat and hiking boots! Let's dive into the heart of America's National Parks and start uncovering 50 of the most fascinating facts they have to offer!

- Did you know that there are 63 national parks in the United States? These natural wonders cover 3.4 percent of the country and span 84.6 million acres of land.

- The world's first national park is Yellowstone National Park, established in 1872. It's so immense that it stretches across three states—Montana, Wyoming, and Idaho. Covering a massive 3,472 square miles, it surpasses the combined area of Delaware and Rhode Island put together!

- Yellowstone National Park has over 500 geysers - that's about half of all the geysers in the world! Sitting on a dormant volcano, it's also the home of the renowned Old Faithful geyser, which puts on a show for us every 91 minutes. That means this geyser has erupted over a million times since Yellowstone became a national park!

Yellowstone National Park

- In the wilds of Yellowstone National Park, you'll discover a unique flower called the Yellowstone Sand-verbena. This little beauty is adorned with tiny white blossoms, brightening the park when it blooms in mid-June. It's a one-of-a-kind flower you won't find anywhere else on our planet!

- Yellowstone National Park's Grand Prismatic Spring, is the largest hot spring in the park, where you can witness a pool that looks like a rainbow come to life. Captivating bands of orange, yellow, and green set against the deep blue waters for a mesmerizing sight. The presence of diverse thermophilic bacteria creates these stunning colors.

- The deepest lake in the United States is Crater Lake in Oregon. It is also known as one of the most pristine lakes on Earth. Here, you will meet the Old Man. He is a 30-foot hemlock log with three feet exposed above water that has been bobbing around vertically in the lake since at least 1896.

- Crater Lake is a source of mystery for scientists because no one knows where the water goes! Its precipitation rates are way higher than its evaporation rates, and there are no outlets to other water sources, so a considerable quantity of water is unaccounted for.

Crater Lake National Park

- Arches National Park in Utah is the ultimate playground of natural stone sculptures of all shapes and sizes. There are over 2,000 arches, which are basically nature's handmade bridges. That's more arches than anywhere else in the world! At this park, you'll also discover pinnacles, balanced rocks, and fins—rock art formed by the Earth's creative forces of the past.

- Everglades National Park in Florida is home to the American Alligator. These creatures can reach lengths of over 16 feet and live up to 35 years. Even more interesting is that as an alligator's teeth wear down, they keep getting new ones! During their lifetime, an alligator can go through a jaw-dropping 3,000 teeth!

- Everglades National Park in Florida is a one-of-a-kind habitat for animal life. Because of a unique blend of freshwater from Lake Okeechobee and saltwater from the ocean, it's the only place on Earth where alligators and crocodiles can live together.

Everglades National Park

- The Grand Canyon in Arizona has been forming for about 6 million years, sculpted by the patient hand of the Colorado River. It averages 4,000 feet deep, with its deepest point being 6,000 feet. This world-famous canyon is also on the list of the Seven Natural Wonders of the World.

- Yosemite Falls in Yosemite National Park stretches up to 2,425 feet tall. It's one of the tallest waterfalls in North America! Yosemite Falls is made up of three separate cascades—the Upper Yosemite Fall plunges at 1,430 feet, followed by the Middle Cascades at 675 feet, and finally, the Lower Yosemite Fall, which cascades down 320 feet.

- On clear spring nights when the moon is shining brightly, there's a chance you might witness an extraordinary sight—a rare lunar rainbow, often called a "moonbow." This enchanting phenomenon is created by the moonlight bending and dancing in the mist created by Yosemite Falls in Yosemite National Park.

Yosemite Falls in Yosemite National Park

- In Utah's Bryce Canyon National Park, you'll find something very unique - tall, slender rock spires created by powerful erosion called "hoodoos". Hoodoos can be as small as the size of an average person to as massive as a 10-story building! These interesting rock formations took shape between 70 and 75 million years ago during the Cretaceous Period. This park is a rock sculpture garden carved by time!

- On the Big Island of Hawaii, you can explore Hawaii Volcanoes National Park, which is home to two active volcanoes: Kilauea and Mauna Loa. Mauna Loa is the world's largest above-ground mountain, stretching 70 miles from one end to another. Below the ocean's surface, it reaches 16,500 feet to the sea floor, making it even taller than Mount Everest from base to peak.

- Hawaii Volcanoes National Park showcases black sand beaches created by volcanic activity. Here, you can witness molten lava flowing into the ocean or a magical evening lava glow under the starry night sky.

Hawaii Volcanoes National Park

- Yellowstone National Park is one of the only places in the United States where bison can roam around as they please. Bison have been living here continuously since dinosaur times!

- In Colorado's Great Sand Dunes National Park and Preserve, the sand dunes will sing a song for you! Just like we make sounds by moving air through our vocal cords, the dunes hum when the wind pushes millions of tiny sand grains during a mini-avalanche. You can even make it happen by driving sand down a dune yourself! It's like nature's own musical instrument.

- The highest peak in North America is in Denali National Park in Alaska. At a towering height of 20,310 feet above sea level, Denali is ranked the third-highest among the Seven Summits, which are the tallest peaks on each of the seven continents.

Denali National Park

- The tallest tree in the world is the Hyperion, a coastal redwood tree. It stands tall at 379 feet and lives in the heart of Redwood National Park in California. The second tallest tree, Helios, and the third tallest, Icarus, also live in this national park.

- The largest national park in the U.S. is in Alaska. Wrangell–St. Elias National Park has 9 million acres of land, making it larger than Switzerland! The park is home to over 100 named glaciers, including the Malaspina Glacier, the largest Piedmont glacier in North America.

- One national park you will want to visit when it is damp and rainy is the Olympic National Park in Washington. Here, you'll find the Hoh Rainforest, famous for its giant mosses and trees draped in vibrant green moss. Rainy and wet weather brings out the best of this lush greenery. You're also more likely to spot a banana slug, the world's second-largest land slug.

Olympic National Park

- Mammoth Cave National Park in Kentucky has the most extended cave system known to man, with over 400 miles of passages explored. This cave system is home to a rare and endangered creature known as the Kentucky cave shrimp, which only exists here. These little crustaceans have see-through bodies, no eyes, and can grow to about an inch long. They're like nature's hidden treasure, living deep, deep underground.

- If you want an adventure, you can sled down the tallest sand dune in North America at Great Sand Dunes National Park in Colorado. The huge 755-foot dune, known as Star Dune, is a dream come true for thrill-seekers who crave the need for speed!

- California's Sequoia National Park is where you'll find General Sherman, the grandest tree known to mankind. With a massive volume of 52,500 cubic feet, it's definitely the most enormous tree around, and scientists even believe this relatively young tree is still growing!

Sequoia National Park

- Uncover ancient fossils in Petrified Forest National Park in Arizona. This park has preserved fossils from the Late Triassic Period, often called the "dawn of the dinosaurs," when these creatures first appeared— even before the Jurassic Period. This was over 200 million years ago!

- Petrified Forest National Park is a museum of ancient trees that have transformed into stone over millions of years. The logs you'll discover look like giant crystals, nearly solid quartz, glistening brilliantly in the sunlight.

- In the Great Smoky Mountains National Park, you'll get to see nature's own synchronized dance party during firefly mating season! These unique fireflies light up all together—some have a yellow-green glow, while others shine in blue or white. The boy fireflies usually flash while they fly around, and the girl fireflies stay in one place and flash back.

Great Smoky Mountains National Park

- Enjoy a boat ride in the Kenai Fjords National Park of Alaska and see giant glaciers breaking apart and falling into the water with a big splash. This is called "glacier calving," and the thunderous sound can be heard for miles and miles!

- Mesa Verde National Park is a remarkable place of history and mystery. Here, you can discover over 4,000 archaeological sites and 600 cliff dwellings. The Ancestral Pueblo people called this place home for about 700 years until they left suddenly, leaving behind these incredible sites for us to explore and wonder about.

- Biscayne National Park in Florida is an underwater forest, with 95% of the park's nearly 173,000 acres found underwater. Besides the area near the visitor center, a boat is needed to experience this national park to the fullest. Once you're there, it's like diving into a different world— you can explore the colorful coral reefs, discover shipwrecks, and see all kinds of ocean creatures.

Biscayne National Park

- One of the hottest spots on the planet was recorded in a national park! Back in 1913, the temperature in Death Valley National Park, which stretches across California and Nevada, reached a scorching 134°F. Even today, it frequently sizzles at around 120°F in Death Valley. It's a real hot spot!

- Angels Landing in Zion National Park is known as one of the most daring hikes in the world. Despite its short length of 2.5 miles, it challenges hikers with a steep 1,500-foot elevation climb. However, most of those who conquer this thrilling hike will agree that the breathtaking views make every heart-pounding moment worth it!

- Zion National Park in Utah has a hike called "The Narrows," where you walk in a river surrounded by towering cliffs on both sides. These awe-inspiring vertical sandstone walls reach 2,000 feet, making it a journey through a canyon of giants!

Zion National Park

- Back in the 1880s, Mormon settlers in Utah's Capitol Reef National Park planted extensive fruit orchards in a place known as Fruita. Today, visitors have the privilege to savor the sweet fruits of their labor during harvest season!

- Shenandoah National Park in Virginia has a unique history. It's not just known for its pristine natural beauty; people lived here for over a century. To bring this park to life, state officials purchased privately owned tracts and donated the land to the country. When it was time to clear the land, they allowed elderly and disabled folks to stay in the park until they passed away. The last person to call this park home died in 1979 at 92 years of age.

- Big Bend gets its name from a dramatic bend in the Rio Grande River that marks its border. This national park boasts the darkest night skies in the whole country, making it one of the top spots for stargazing!

Big Bend National Park

- Theodore Roosevelt National Park in North Dakota is the only national park named after a person. This park is a living tribute to the 26th president of the United States, Theodore Roosevelt, who had a deep connection with this land even before becoming president. He would later help create the U.S. Forest Service, an organization committed to safeguarding the nation's forests.

- You'll discover Carlsbad Caverns National Park in New Mexico, a vast network of hidden caves and chambers. One of the breathtaking formations you will find here is known as the "Big Room," an underground chamber so huge that it has its very own weather system.

- Underground in Wind Cave National Park, endless secrets are waiting to be discovered, as only about 5% of it has been explored. This is the first cave to be named a national park in the world, as well as one of the longest ones, covering about 44 square miles. In 1881, two brothers in South Dakota stumbled across a hole in a rock with wind gushing out. That's how this park got its name.

- Joshua Tree National Park is famous for its Joshua trees, but here's a surprising fact: Joshua trees aren't really trees at all! They're a type of yucca plant that can reach heights of up to 40 feet, and they have been used for centuries for weaving baskets, thanks to their sturdy leaves.

Joshua Tree National Park

- Indiana Dunes National Park is among the freshest additions to the national park family, earning its status in 2019. It's also one of the most biologically diverse national parks. Inside its borders, you'll discover an impressive array of over 1,100 species of flowering plants and ferns.

- The Channel Islands National Park off the coast of California is home to the highest number of nesting bald eagles in the lower 48 states. Bald eagles are an integral part of the island's ecosystem.

- Badlands National Park in South Dakota has a fascinating history. During World War II, part of this rugged landscape was used as a practice bombing range. After the war, the South Dakota National Guard used portions as an artillery range. The Air Force still retains a small portion, but it is no longer in use. The memory of its wartime adventures still echoes in the rocks and canyons.

Badlands National Park

- In the Northeast, there's a special place called Acadia National Park in Maine, and it's the one and only national park in this part of the country. Acadia is mainly known for a natural inlet carved by the rocks called Thunder Hole. You can experience the mighty roar of the sea here as crashing waves slam against the rugged shoreline!

- The Chisos Mountains, stretching 20 miles, stand proudly at the heart of Big Bend National Park in Texas. It's the only mountain range wholly enclosed within a single national park!

- Dry Tortugas National Park is the most remote national park, located 70 miles from Key West, Florida. This park is home to the third-largest coral barrier reef in the world and the only tropical reef in the continental U.S. Its name stems from two factors. First, there's no source of fresh water within the park, so they called it "dry." Second, "Tortugas" is the Spanish word for turtle, and you'll find five different types of turtles living within the park.

Dry Tortugas National Park

- Gateway Arch National Park in Missouri may be the tiniest national park, just 91 acres, but it's different from your typical nature-packed park. Here, you'll find the famous Gateway Arch, which commemorates the Louisiana Purchase and the westward exploration of the U.S. in the 18th century.

- The Gateway Arch is also the tallest monument in the United States, at a whopping 630 feet tall and wide. In 1948, a nationwide design competition was held to decide what shape the Memorial would take. The winner was a creative architect named Eero Saarinen. He dreamt up this unique design for a gleaming stainless steel arch, and in 1963, they started building it. The Arch resembles a shining, silver rainbow reaching high into the sky.

- At Glacier National Park in Montana, there's a unique way to check out the scenic views. Visitors can take a ride in vintage red buses called "Jammers." These particular buses made their debut at the park in the 1930s in an effort to reduce traffic.

The name comes from when you could hear the manual transmission grind on the steeper slopes, but don't worry—they have been renovated since then! With the top pulled back, you get the best view as you ride along the world-famous winding Going-to-the-Sun Road. You'll feel like you're stepping into a postcard brought to life.

Glacier National Park

Young explorers, the world of national parks is a magical place to discover the deepest canyons, climb the tallest peaks, and witness nature's grandeur in all its glory.

Picture yourself marveling at the geysers in Yellowstone, standing humbly in front of General Sherman, or peering down into the immense depths of the Grand Canyon.

The national parks are more than just facts. They are exciting experiences, huge discoveries, and unforgettable memories with family and friends. Pack your bags—adventure is calling!

Made in the USA
Las Vegas, NV
27 November 2023